The Wonders of
SCIENCE

by Bertha Morris Parker

formerly of the Laboratory Schools,
University of Chicago; Research Associate,
Chicago Natural History Museum

pictures by Kelly Oechsli

GOLDEN PRESS • NEW YORK

distributed by

ENCYCLOPÆDIA BRITANNICA

CHICAGO

A Pinwheel

1970 EDITION

© Copyright 1963 by Western Publishing Company, Inc.
All rights reserved.
Printed in the U.S.A. by Western Publishing Company, Inc.
Library of Congress Catalog Card Number: 63-17546.

Make a pinwheel.
Cut a five-inch square of paper
    and color it on one side.
The pictures show you
    where to cut the square
    and what corners to fold in.

Stick a big pin
    through the center
    and into the eraser of a new pencil.
Hold the pinwheel out in front
    of you and run.
Watch it whirl around.
The air strikes the blades
    and makes them turn.

An "Empty Bottle"

Get an empty bottle.
Hold it sideways in a deep pan or bowl
  full of water.
Watch the bubbles come up.
The bubbles are air.
An empty bottle isn't really empty.
It is full of air.

Blowing Over a Tin Can

Stand a tin can on a table.
Try to blow it over.
You will find you can't.
But there is a way of blowing it over.
Fasten a balloon to the end of a straw.
Lay the balloon on the table
  and stand the tin can on it.
Then blow into the straw.
The balloon will swell up
  and make the tin can fall over.

Blowing Water Out of a Bottle

An Experiment with a Rubber Bulb

Put four inches of water in a dishpan.
Lay a milk bottle in it on its side.
When the bottle is full of water,
  stand it upside down
  in the dishpan.
The water will stay in.
Now use a straw or a rubber tube to blow
  out the water in the bottle.

Take the rubber bulb off the end
  of a medicine dropper.
Squeeze the air out of it and put
  the rim against the back
  of your hand.
Let go of the bulb.
It should stay on your hand.
The air outside holds it on.

Here is a toy you can make.

Cut out a fish from an old balloon.

Fill a milk bottle nearly full of water.

Make two small holes in the cap
  of the bottle.

Push a drinking straw through one hole
  and a funnel through the other.

Use sticky tape to make the cap airtight.

Put the fish in the funnel.

The poor fish has no water to swim in.

Give it some by blowing in the straw.

The air you blow into the bottle
  will push some of the water
  up into the top of the funnel.

Making Water Run Uphill

Stand two glasses side by side.
Fill one with water.

Cut a strip about an inch wide
  from an old bath towel.
Put one end in one glass and
  the other in the other glass.
Let the glasses stand overnight.

Water will travel slowly through the cloth
  from one glass to the other.

Fill a rubber tube with water
  and hold both ends shut.
Put one end in the bowl and
  the other in the sink.
Let go of the ends.
Water will rush through the tube
  up over the edge of the bowl
  and down into the sink.
A tube used in this way
  is called a siphon.

Fill a big bowl with water and
  stand it on the drainboard
  of the kitchen sink.

Air pushing down on the water in the bowl
makes the siphon work.

There are many kinds of kites.
A kite may have a tail.
The tail helps to hold the kite
in the right position.

Flying a Kite

Try flying a kite on a warm day
   when there is a little breeze.
To fly a kite you run into the breeze.
The wind pushing on the underside
   of the kite makes it rise.
At first hold the string close
   to the kite.
Let the string slip through
   your fingers as the kite rises.

Experimenting with a Glider

Fold a sheet of typewriter paper
  to make a glider.
The pictures show you how.
Throw the glider into the air.
Air under the wings
  will make it glide down to the ground
  instead of falling straight down.
Now, instead of throwing the glider
  into the air,
  hold it from above
  and let it fall.
Notice that the nose hits
  the ground first.

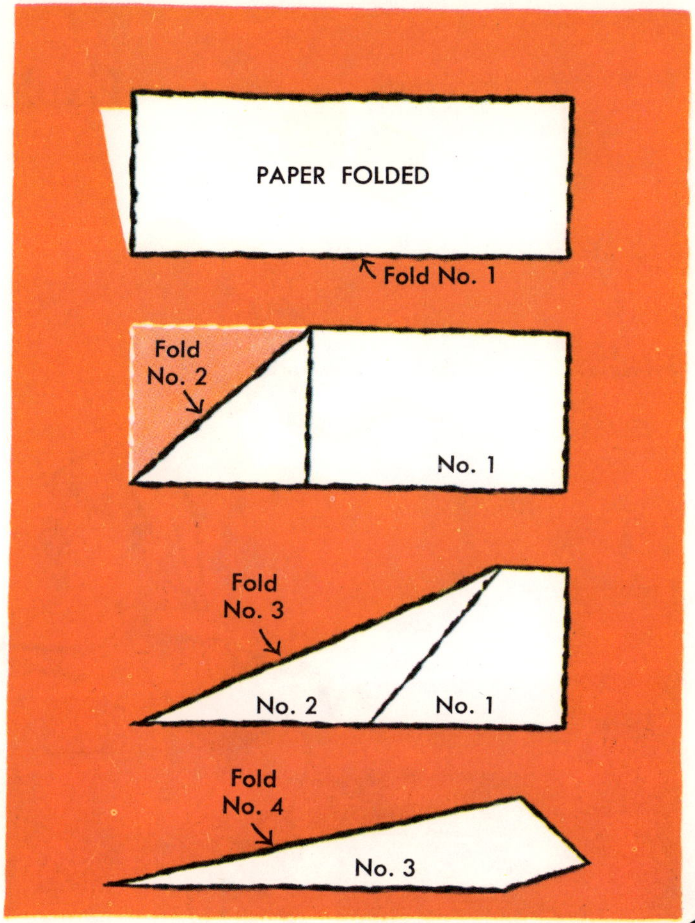

There is much more wing
  at the back than at the front
  for the air to push up against.

Exploring

Go exploring in your back yard
  or in a park.
You may find some pretty pebbles,
  a flower with a pleasant smell,

a robin hunting for a worm,
a ladybug on a leaf,
a fuzzy caterpillar,

a spider web,
a flower bud just opening,
or something else just as interesting.

Raising Flowers Indoors

Get a flat bowl, some pebbles,
  and six paper-white narcissus bulbs.

Put the bulbs in the bowl
  and pack pebbles around them.
The pebbles will hold the bulbs in place.
Pour in enough water
  to cover the pebbles.

Keep the bowl in a dark place
  for a day or two.
Then put it in a sunny window.
The bulbs will grow and bloom
  if you keep giving them
  the water they need.

A Pretty Green Plant for Indoors

Cut a carrot in two
  and stand the upper half
  in a small dish.
Hold it in place with pebbles.
Pour in enough water
  to cover the pebbles.
Leaves will grow from the top
  of the piece of carrot.
Carrot leaves are feathery
  and very pretty.

A Garden in a Fish Bowl

Make a garden in a fish bowl.
Put a little soil in the bowl.
Cover it with a layer of moss.
Add a tiny fern or two and a
  plant with bright-colored berries.
Make the moss very damp.
Cover the bowl with a plate of glass.
The plate of glass will keep
  the garden from drying out fast.
You will not have to water it often.

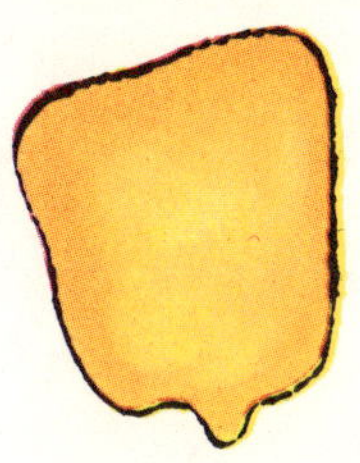   

Taking Seeds Apart

Get some large seeds
  of different kinds.
Soak them in water overnight.

Then open them up and look
  for the tiny plants inside.
Every seed has in it a baby plant
  and some food for the little plant.

Finding Seeds in Fruits

Open some fruits
and see how many seeds
each one has in it.
Count them if you can.

Experiments with Seeds

Put some radish seeds on a wet blotter
in a clear plastic container
with a lid.
The seeds will sprout.
Look at them each day.
Notice the little brushes of root hairs
on the roots.
Water gets into the little plants
through these root hairs.

Plant some bush balsam seeds
in a pot in a sunny window.
Bush balsam will grow and bloom
in pots indoors.
The flowers will produce seed pods.
If you touch a ripe balsam seed pod,
it will shoot out its seeds.
Another name for bush balsam
is touch-me-not.

More Experiments with Seeds

Fold a paper towel, roll it up,
 and stand it in a glass.
Put some bean seeds between the towel
 and the glass.
The towel will hold them in place.
Pour a little water into the glass.
It will soak up into the towel.
The bean seeds will sprout and grow.
Add water from time to time.

In the summer
 find a ripe dandelion head
 and blow the seeds away.
In the fall
 find a milkweed pod
 that has split open.
Blow the seeds in it away.

A Tiny Greenhouse

Early in the spring
  fill a pot with soil
  and plant some seeds in it.
Dampen the soil well.
Turn a glass jar upside down
  over the soil.
Put the pot outdoors in a sunny spot.
Heat from the sunshine
  will be trapped by the glass jar.
The seeds in your little greenhouse
  should sprout and grow.

Does Grass Need Light?

Some summer day
  turn a flowerpot upside down
  on the grass
  in your yard.
Put the flowerpot
  where no one will stumble
  over it.
After a few days look and see
  what has happened
  to the grass underneath.
Grass needs light.

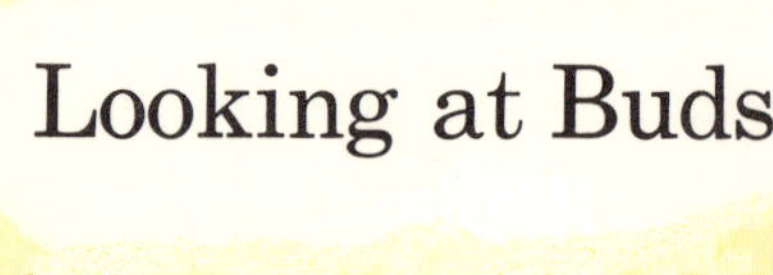

Looking at Buds

After the leaves have fallen in the fall,
cut twigs from different kinds
of trees and bushes.
Look at the buds on the twigs.
You will find that every bud
is covered with brown scales.
Most buds you find in the fall
are leaf buds.
A few are flower buds.
Open some of the buds with a toothpick.

In the early spring
cut a few twigs from bushes and trees
and bring them indoors.
Stand them in a jar of water.
Watch to see what happens to the buds.

In the summer
look for flower buds.
Take one bud apart to see
how the parts of the flower
are folded up inside.

Pets

Here are some animals
  that make good pets.
Visit a pet store and see
  what other animals they sell for pets.
If you have any pets
  be sure you give them
  the kind of care they need.
Find out what kinds of food
  are best for them.
Keep their cages
  or pens or other places
  where they stay clean.

Animals with Shells

Pick up a little turtle.
See whether it pulls its head
and legs inside its shell.

Pick up a snail.
See whether it pulls its body
inside its shell.

Watching

Watch for birds in your back yard.
Draw a colored picture of each kind
  you see.

If you have a flower garden,
  hummingbirds may visit it.
So may honeybees and bumblebees
  and butterflies.
Watch for garden visitors.

More Watching

On a summer evening
   catch some fireflies and put them
   in a glass jar with a lid.
Watch them light up.
After you have watched a while,
   take off the lid
   and let them fly away.

In the spring
   watch for baby animals.
There are many animal babies
   in the spring.

Feeding Wild Birds

In the winter
  put out some food for birds
  on a feeding shelf.
Cracked corn, suet, apples, and bread
  are some foods birds eat.
At your grocery store
  you may be able to buy wild bird seed
  for your shelf.

Collecting Leaves and Pebbles

Make a leaf collection.
Fall is a good time to begin
  because many leaves change color then.

Try to find pretty red leaves
  and yellow leaves and green leaves
  and brown leaves.

Make a pile of sheets of newspaper
  and put the leaves between the sheets.
Put some heavy books on top of the pile
  to press the leaves flat.
After two or three days mount them
  in a scrapbook with sticky tape.

Make a collection of pretty pebbles.

Collecting Seeds and Shells

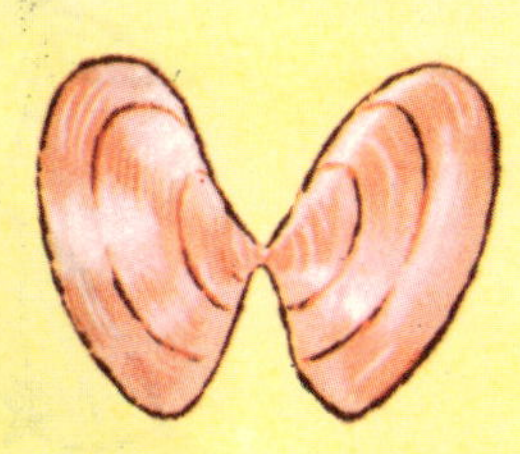

Make a seed collection.
Fall is a good time to start.
You will find seeds
   of many different shapes and sizes.
Put the different kinds of seeds
   in little boxes or in envelopes.
Cellophane envelopes are very good
   for small seeds.

Make a collection of seashells
   if you have a chance.
Summer is a good time
   to go to a seashore
   and look for shells.
Try to find shells of different sizes
   that are alike in other ways.
Sort out your shells.
Put in one box the two-piece shells
   that close up like a pocketbook.
Put the one-piece shells
   in another box.

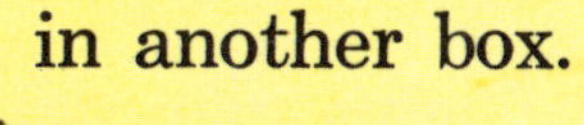

Using Your Senses

Have someone blindfold you.
Then have him hand you things to feel.
Try to tell what each one is.

You can play the same game
   with sounds.
Crumpling paper does not sound
   like tapping on wood.
A whistle does not sound like a drum.

Try playing the same game with smells.
Of course, many things do not have
   any smell.
The person you are playing with
   should hold each thing
   you are to smell
   near your nose.
You should not take it in your hands.
Its feel might give it away.

Seeing through a Book

Roll a sheet of writing paper
   into a roll about an inch across.
Hold it up to your right eye.
Hold a book in front of your left eye.
Look at a picture on the wall.
You will seem to be looking
   through a hole in the book.

You see the book with one eye,
   and with the other eye
   you see the picture
   through the tube.

Fun with a Mirror

Stand a little mirror up
  on the red line of the ball.
Do you still see a ball?

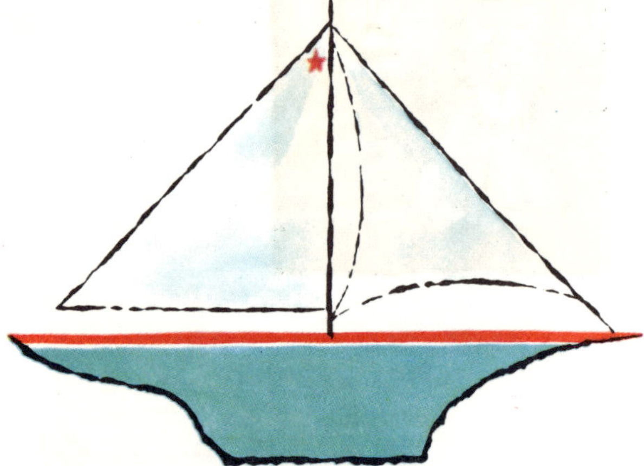

Stand the mirror up
  on the red line of the boat.
Do you still see a boat?

Hold a small mirror in the sunshine.
Pick out some place
  you want the light to strike.
Move your mirror till it sends
  a bright spot of light there.

Reflections

Get two square pocketbook mirrors.
Stand a pin up in a piece
  of cardboard.
Stand the mirrors up on each side
  of the pin.
Bend them up toward each other.
You will see a wheel of pins
  in the mirrors.

Look at yourself in the bowl
  of a shiny silver spoon.
Look first on the inside
  and then on the outside.
Do you look the same in the two sides?

Shadow Pictures

At night throw shadow pictures
  on the wall.
You will need a bright lamp
  not very far from a light wall.
Turn out the other lights in the room.
Notice that you change the size
  of the shadows by changing
  your distance from the wall.

In the daytime
  you can make shadow pictures
  by using bright sunshine
  coming in a window on a wall.

Stand sideways so that the shadow
  of your head and face falls
  on a big piece of white paper
  on the wall.
Have someone trace your picture.

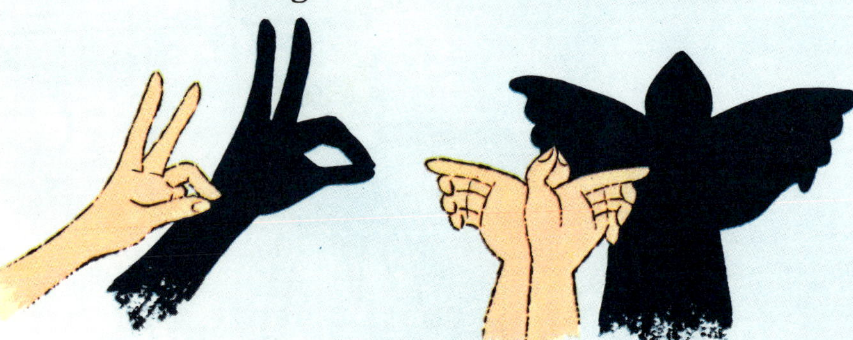

Changing Shadows

Have someone measure your shadow
while you stand in the sunshine
at three different times in one day—

When is your shadow shortest?
When is it longest?

Stand a little doll on a table.
Throw the doll's shadow on the top
of the table with a flashlight.
Find out how you can change the length
and the direction of the shadow.

Fill a small box with modeling clay
and stand a pencil in it.
Put the box in a sunny window.
Look at it several times during a day
and notice that the shadow moves.
Sundials tell time
with moving shadows.

A "Broken" Straw

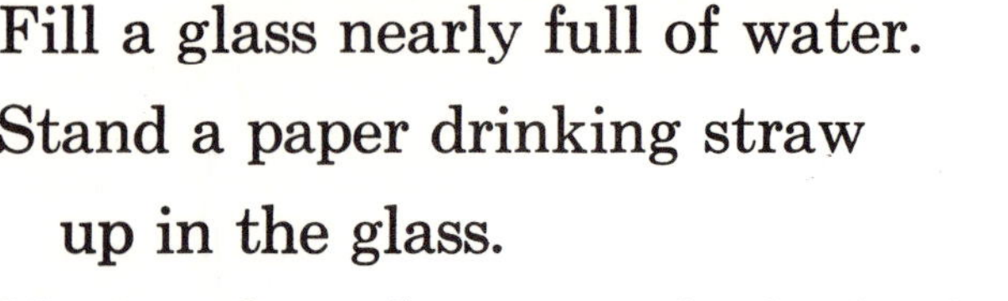

Fill a glass nearly full of water.
Stand a paper drinking straw
  up in the glass.
Notice that the straw looks broken
at the top of the water.
It looks broken because the water
  makes the light bend
  on its way to your eyes.

Making Things Look Bigger

Look at some grains of salt
  through a reading glass.
The reading glass makes them
  look bigger than they are.
It is a magnifying glass.

Get a teaspoonful of dry soil and
  spread it out on a piece of paper.
Look at it through the reading glass.
Are the bits of soil all the same size?

Go exploring by looking at other small things with the reading glass.

Rainbows

Some day when the sun is shining brightly after a shower,
look for a rainbow.

Can you find
red, orange, yellow, green, blue,
and violet in it?
Which color is at the top?

Which one is at the bottom?
Draw a picture with a rainbow in it.
Look for a tiny rainbow in the spray
from a garden sprinkler.

A Rubber-Band Instrument

Get a wooden cigar box
  or a stout cardboard box.
Stretch several narrow rubber bands
  of different lengths around it.
Pluck the rubber bands.
Notice that no two bands
  make exactly the same sound.

Sounds of Living Things

On a summer evening
  sit outdoors very quietly for a while
  and listen for sounds of living things.
You may hear a cricket chirping,
  or leaves rustling, or an owl hooting,
  or a dog barking.
You may hear
  the funny sound a nighthawk makes,
  or the mewing of a kitten,
  or the croak of a frog.

Experiments with Sound

Find a blank wall you can shout at
  and hear the echo.
You should stand at least 50 feet away
  from the wall.

Blow up a paper bag.
Hit it to make it pop.
You make it pop
  by squeezing the air in it.

Make a toy drum
  out of a plastic bowl or tumbler.
Stretch a piece
  of a big rubber balloon
  across the top
  and tie it in place with string.
Unsharpened pencils make
  good drumsticks.

Get a piece of string
    about a yard long.
Tie two spoons to the middle of it.
Hold one end of the string in each hand
    and put the ends up to your ears.

Swing the cord so that the spoons
    strike each other.
They will sound like church bells.
The sound travels up the string
    to your ears.

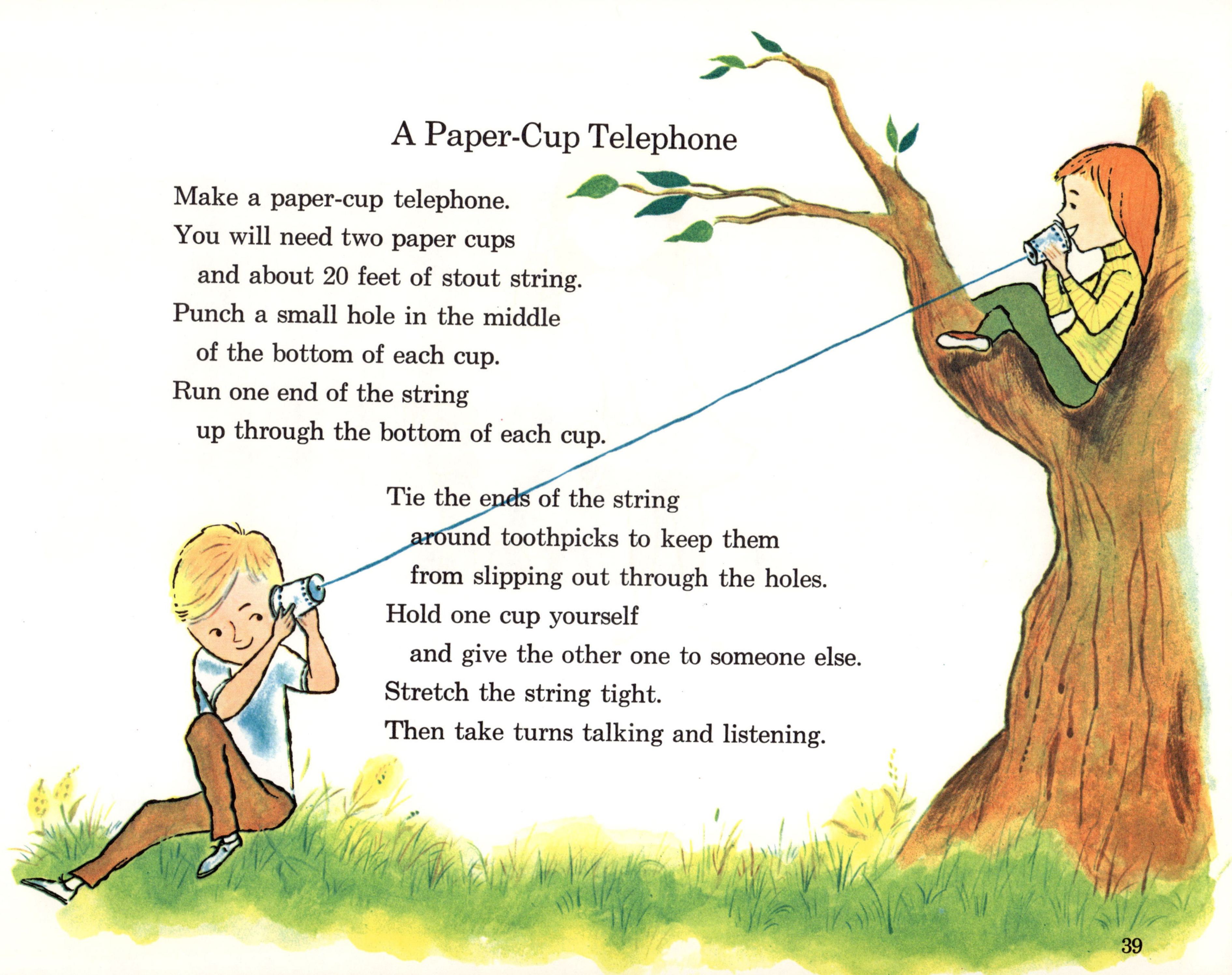

A Paper-Cup Telephone

Make a paper-cup telephone.
You will need two paper cups
  and about 20 feet of stout string.
Punch a small hole in the middle
  of the bottom of each cup.
Run one end of the string
  up through the bottom of each cup.

Tie the ends of the string
  around toothpicks to keep them
  from slipping out through the holes.
Hold one cup yourself
  and give the other one to someone else.
Stretch the string tight.
Then take turns talking and listening.

The Two Dippers

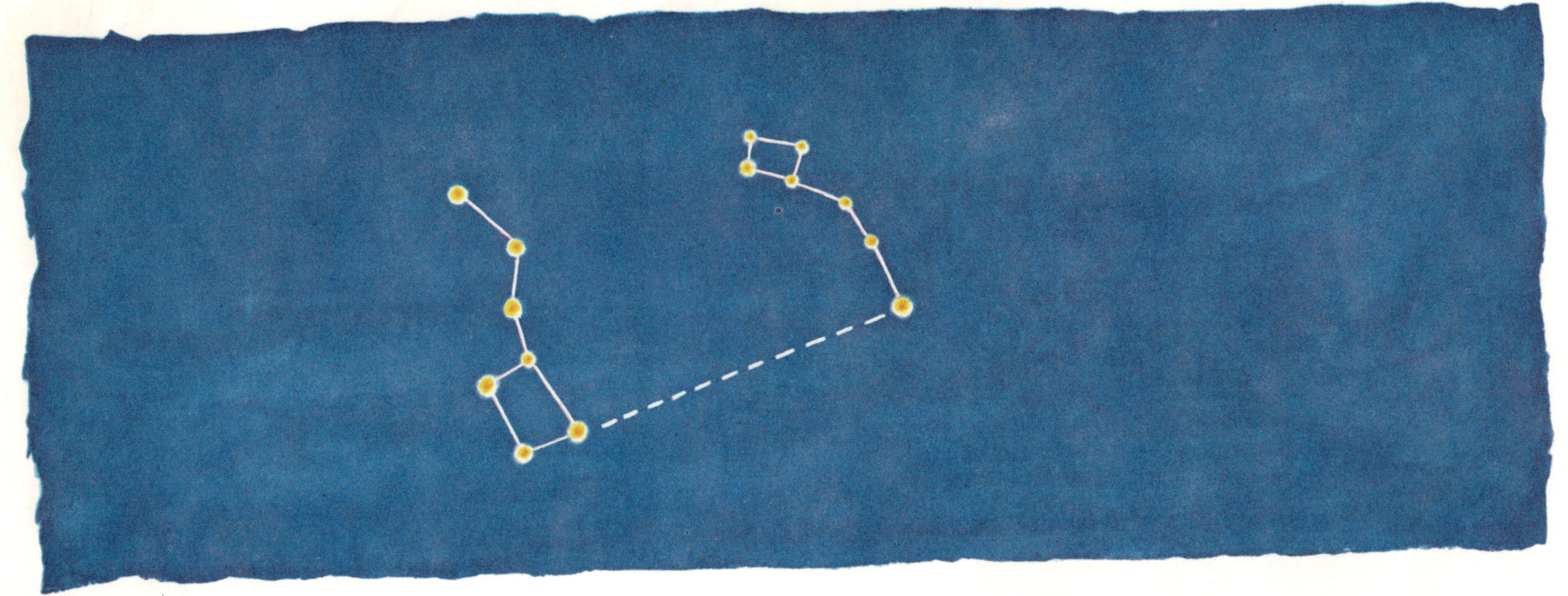

After it gets dark
  look for the Big Dipper
  in the northern sky.
It is made up of bright stars.

Maybe you can find
  the Little Dipper, too.
The stars in it are not very bright.
The North Star is the end of the handle.

The Changing Moon

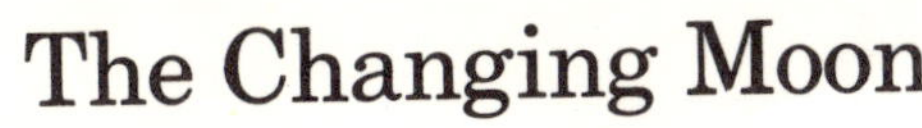

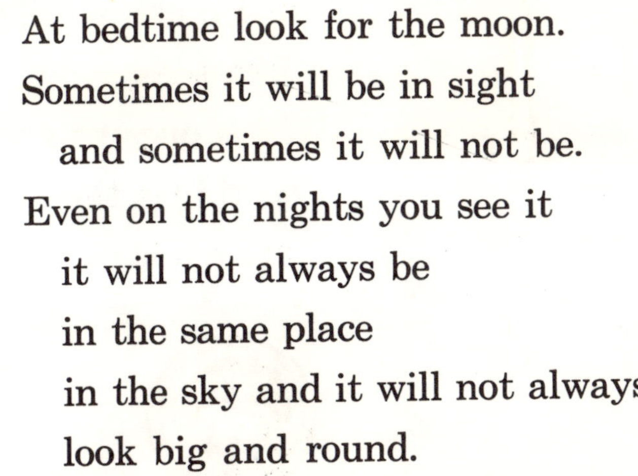

At bedtime look for the moon.
Sometimes it will be in sight
  and sometimes it will not be.
Even on the nights you see it
  it will not always be
  in the same place
  in the sky and it will not always
  look big and round.

Use a yellow crayon to draw a picture
  of the moon the next time you see it.

What Will a Magnet Pick Up?

Get a magnet.
Then make a collection of things
    like these.
Which ones will the magnet pick up?
The things the magnet picks up
    are made of iron or steel.

A Magnet Game

Cut a few fish out of colored paper.

Put a paper clip on the head
  of each fish.

Put the fish in a cardboard box
  with no top.

Make a fishing pole by tying a magnet
  to a pencil with a piece of string.

Go fishing with your fishing pole.

A Paper-Clip Doll

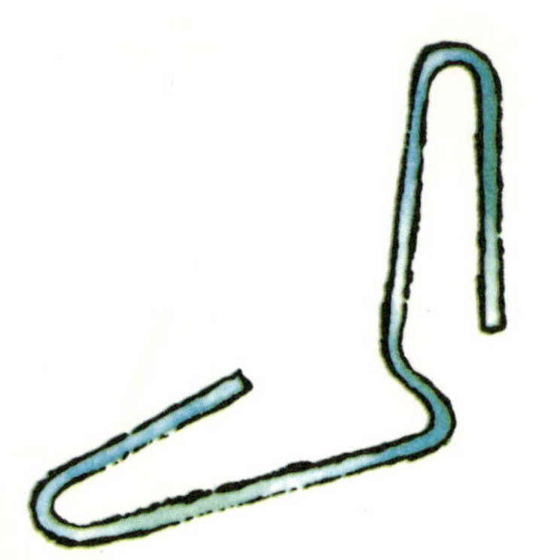

Bend a paper clip up like this:

Cut a paper doll and fasten it
to the bent-up part of the paper clip.

Stand the doll on a card table.
Make the doll move
by moving your magnet around
underneath the table.

A Climbing Paper Clip

A Boat to Pull

Put a paper clip in the bottom
  of a drinking glass
  so that it touches
  the side of the glass.
Use a magnet to make the paper clip
  climb up the side of the glass.

Cut a boat-shaped piece
  of plastic foam.
Cut a paper sail and fasten it
  to the boat with a darning needle.
Float the boat on a pan of water.
Pull it across the water with a magnet.

Electricity from Rubbing

Cut a piece of tissue paper
   into tiny bits.
Rub a rubber or plastic comb
   with a piece of wool.
Pick up bits of the paper
   with the comb.
Rubbing the comb gives it
   a charge of electricity.
The comb picks up the bits of paper
   because it is charged with electricity.

Experiments like this work best
   on a cold, clear day.

Rub a comb
   with a piece of wool.
Make a ping-pong ball roll along a table
   by holding the comb close to it.
The electric charge on the comb pulls
   the ping-pong ball.

Experiments with a Balloon

Blow up a balloon.
Tie the end to hold the air in.
Rub the balloon on the sleeve
  of your coat or sweater.
Then put it against the wall and see
  whether it will stay there.
It will if rubbing it gave it
  a charge of electricity.

Rub a balloon on your hair
  instead of on your sleeve.
Roll up one sleeve,
  and stretch out your arm.
See whether the charged balloon
  will stick to it.

These experiments, too, work best
  on a cold, clear day.

Dancing Dolls

Get a cardboard box
  with a cellophane lid.
Some notepaper
  comes in boxes of this kind.
Cut out a string of paper dolls
  almost as tall as the box is deep.
Stand the dolls up in the box.

Rub the top of the box
  with a handkerchief.
Watch the dolls dance.
Rubbing the box top gives it
  a charge of electricity,
  and the electric charge
  makes the dolls dance.

A Roly-Poly

Make a roly-poly out of an apple,
  a toothpick, and a paper doll.
Cut the apple in half.
Stick the toothpick up straight
  in the center of one half.
Cut out a paper doll
  and paste it to the toothpick.
Push the roly-poly over
  and it will bob up again.
It will bob up because the apple
  is much heavier than the paper doll
  and because the apple is rounded
  at the bottom.

Here is another way to make a roly-poly.
Cut a hollow rubber ball in two.
Fill one half with modeling clay.
Stand a pipe cleaner in the center.
With other pipe cleaners
  make it into a stick man.

Another Roly-Poly

A Balancing Airplane

Follow this pattern
  and cut an airplane
  out of thin cardboard.
With sticky tape
  fasten a penny to the underside
  in the places marked.

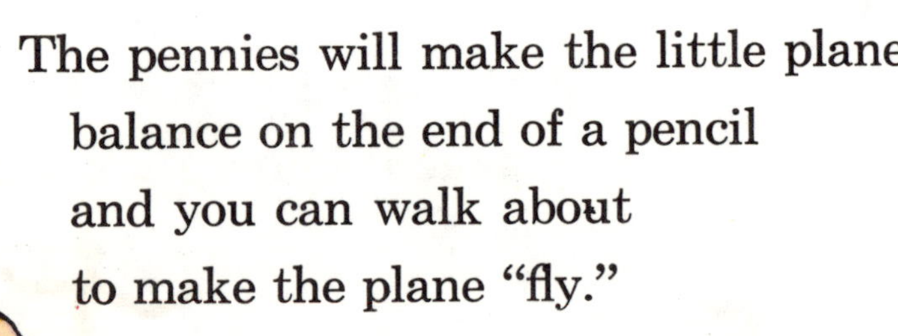

The pennies will make the little plane
  balance on the end of a pencil
  and you can walk about
  to make the plane "fly."

A Dancing Doll

Make a dancing doll.
The pictures show you how.
You will need some cardboard,
  eight brass paper fasteners,
  and some string.

If you pull the string that hangs down,
  the doll will dance.
The top of each arm and leg
  is like a teeter-totter.
When one end goes down, the other goes up.

An Experiment with a Thermometer

Find a thermometer
   that has a red liquid in its tube.
Put your hand on the bulb.
If it is a cool day,
   the warmth of your hand will make
   the red liquid rise in the tube.
Then take your hand away
   and watch the red liquid go down.

Jet Propulsion

Blow up a balloon.
Hold it high.
Then let go of it
   so that the air can rush out.
Watch the balloon shoot away.
The balloon works much
   like a jet airplane.
But in a jet plane
   it is very hot gas that rushes out.

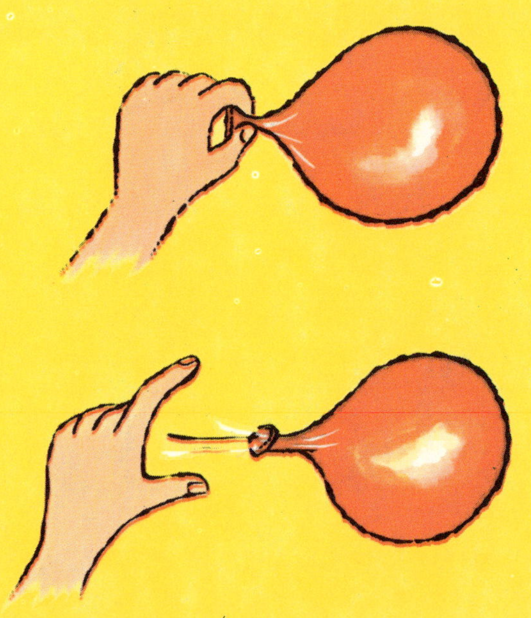

Slope and Speed

Get a toy automobile
  and a smooth board.
Rest one end of the board
  on a low stool.
Put the little car at the top
  of the slope and let it roll down.
Watch to see how fast it goes.

Now move the end of the board
  from the stool
  to the seat of a chair.
Let the little car roll down the slope.
Watch to see how fast it goes.
Does it go faster
  when the slope is steeper?

Floating Ice Cubes

Put two ice cubes in the bottom
  of a tall glass.
Then try to cover the ice cubes
  with water.
You will find that you can't.

The ice cubes will float
  at the top of the water
  that you pour in.
The ice cubes float
  because ice is lighter than water.

Which Will Float?

A Bobbing Toy

Put a toy that will float
in a deep pan or bowl of water.
Push it down to the bottom of the pan
with your hand and watch it bob up
when you let it go.

Sinking a Toy without Touching It

Get some little toy
    that will float on water.
Fill a big pan or bowl nearly full of water
    and put the toy on the surface.
Turn a glass upside down over the toy
    and push the glass down
    till the rim hits the bottom
    of the pan.
The toy will go down, too.
The air in the glass will not let
    the water come in.
The water under the glass goes down,
    and so does the toy floating on it.

Evaporation

Fill a glass nearly full of water.
Put a rubber band around the glass
 at the level of the water.
Then stand the glass aside.
Look at it the next day.
Does the water still come up
 to the rubber band?
Probably not, because some of the water
 will probably have changed to vapor
 and gone up into the air.
Water open to the air evaporates.

Get a mixing bowl, a tall, narrow vase,
 and a big flat pan.
Stand them on a shelf or table.
Pour a cupful of water in each one.
Watch to see which one gets dry first
 and which one gets dry last.

Which Dries First?

Get two pieces of cloth just alike.
Put them both in water
 and then wring them both out
 as dry as you can.
Leave one crumpled up on a plate.
Open the other one out
 and hang it up to dry.
Which one dries first?

Wet the two pieces of cloth again.
Hang one in bright sunshine
 and the other in the shade.
Which one dries first?

Paint a circle with water paint
 on each of two pieces of paper.
Leave one piece on a table.
Hold the other in front of a fan.
Which one dries first?

Dissolving

Put a teaspoonful of sugar in a glass.
Then pour some drinking water
  into the glass.
Stir the sugar and watch it.
Soon it will disappear.
But it is still there.
Taste the water and see.
The sugar dissolves in the water.

Try to dissolve a teaspoonful of flour
  in a glass of water.
Does it dissolve?

Dissolve a teaspoonful of salt
  in a cup of water.
Then pour the water into a pie pan
  and leave it to evaporate.
When the water evaporates,
  the salt is left behind.

On a windy day look for clouds
  moving across the sky.
Watch them change shape
  as the wind blows them along.

Watch for pretty sunsets.
If there are clouds high in the sky
  when the sun goes down,
  the sunset may be beautiful.

Dew and Frost

On a summer morning
  look for dew on flowers
  and spider webs.

On a cool fall day
  look for frost on the grass
  and on roofs.

On a cold winter day
  look for frost on windows.

An Experiment with Snow

On a snowy day fill a cup with snow.
Bring it indoors where it is warm.
The snow will melt
  and soon there will be nothing
  but water in the cup.
But the cup will not be full of water.
It would take about ten cupfuls of snow
  to make one cupful of water.